Dropping Gemz™ Book Series
Book 2

Holistic Gemz

How to treat seasonal and year-long allergies naturally

Keisha Christian

Dropping Gemz Publishing
218-10 Merrick Blvd.
Unit 130474
Springfield Gardens, NY 11413
www.keishagemz.com

Copyright © 2019 by Keisha Christian
All rights reserved.

All rights reserved. No part of this book may be reproduced in any form by electronic or mechanical means, including information storage and retrieval systems, without permission in writing from the publisher. The only exception is for a reviewer, who may quote brief passages in a book review.

ISBN: 978-1-7325788-1-4

DISCLAIMER

The herbal cures in this book are my own observations and opinions; they should not be taken as professional medical advice. You are responsible for performing your own research, as every individual circumstance differs. If you put any of the suggestions in this book into action, you are entirely responsible for the results. By continuing to read this book, you agree with the terms and conditions herein expressed.

All reproduced work must refer to the author. Please feel free to share this book with anyone you choose. You may send it to colleagues or friends, give it as a gift, and even post it on your blog, so long as you agree not to edit, re-create, or personalize it.

If you are under a doctor's care for your allergies or other health concerns, please discuss any new supplements or practices. This is especially true if you are taking medication for your allergies or other conditions. You may find that natural remedies are able to help manage, soothe, or eliminate your allergies: that is the essence of this book.

Remember to take care of yourself: you are worth it!

Dropping Gemz™ Book Series
Book 1

Available on Amazon
www.amazon.com/author/keishachristian

Autographed copy available
www.keishagemz.com/books

> *Take care of your body.*
> *It's the only place you*
> *have to live.*
> *-Jim Rohn*

How are you?

Seriously. Just take a moment, pause, and listen to yourself. Check in with your body. Are you struggling with the painful effects of your allergies? I know that seasonal and year-long allergies take their toll, as I have dealt with them since I was a child. Over the years, through trial and error, I discovered ways to curb many of the difficult symptoms allergies can create.

This short book will introduce you to simple tools, renewing practices, and little luxuries that help manage your allergies and boost your immune system. They will support you in starting a conversation with your body, as the wisdom of our bodies connects us to our true selves and our internal guidance system.

I invite you to explore, to be curious and playful with the tools in this book. You don't have to do everything all at once. All you have to do is begin, right where you are. Choose something that speaks to you and spend just a few minutes at it. A simple act of self-care can serve as a pattern interruption, providing love and nourishment to your whole being. Start the journey, even with the smallest step; the brilliance of your being is waiting.

Peace and Blessings,

Keisha

UNDERSTANDING ALLERGIES

It is estimated that 50 million people in the United States suffer from some kind of allergy[1]. As the 6th leading cause of chronic illness in the U.S., allergies can be triggered by almost anything in our environment, such as food, medications, pollen, pollution, and more.

Our immune system protects us from disease by killing foreign substances that can make us sick, such as viruses and bacteria. An allergic reaction occurs when our immune system makes a mistake and "overreacts" to a benign substance.[2] When this happens, we call that substance an "allergen."

Once the immune system has identified a threat, it tries to remove the intruder and heal damaged tissues. One way the body does this is by releasing histamine, which creates inflammation that causes blood vessels to expand and become more permeable. This allows white blood cells, antibodies, and other immune system liquids to move from the bloodstream to injured or infected tissues. The familiar symptoms of congestion, watering eyes, swollen ears, and upset stomach often accompany this process.

All allergies can be helped by strengthening the immune system so it is less likely to react to a harmless substance. For some allergies, the best way to manage them is to avoid the irritant, if possible. For example, if you are allergic to cow's milk, you eliminate dairy from your diet and that solves the problem. Unfortunately, avoidance is not always possible, such as with airborne allergens like pollen. In these instances, we can try to reduce our exposure, and then strengthen and soothe our bodies so we are more comfortable.

It is important in your self-care journey to seek practices that resonate with you. Be aware that if you have any sort of allergy, your immune system is already working harder than usual. You may be sensitive to the herbs, oils, or other ingredients in the suggestions contained here. Please recognize that you are an individual deserving the best of care, which means discussing any new practices or supplements with your doctor.

This book provides tools that can help strengthen your immune system and reduce the stress that any allergy can create. While there are many different types of allergies, I focus on seasonal and year-long allergies, such as pollen or mold. Regardless of what type of allergy you may have, focus on the immune-building and soothing practices in this book. Strengthening your entire being will provide gradual relief and respite from the challenges allergies present. Have patience—over time you will develop healthy habits that reduce your symptoms.

Contents

Chapter 1: Nasal Irrigation Device 1
Chapter 2: Essential Oils 7
   Oil of Oregano Recipe for immune boosting 15
   Recipe for Digestive Health & Respiratory System 17
   Recipe for the Skin 18
Chapter 3: Bentonite Clay 19
   Calcium Bentonite Clay Tonic Recipe 24
Chapter 4: Water 25
   Citrus Infused Water Recipe 30
   Cucumber Mint Water 31
   Cucumber Lemon Water Recipe 32
   Watermelon Citrus Water 33
   Oregano Rosemary Watermelon Infused Water 34
Chapter 5: Probiotic & Fermented Foods 35
   Fermented Chia Pudding Recipe 40
   Rejuvelac Recipe 41
Chapter 6: Nuts & Seeds 43
   Basic Nut & Seed Milk Recipe 49
Chapter 7: Spices & Herbs 51
   Apple Ginger Juice Recipe 57
   Golden Milk Recipe 58
Chapter 8: Microgreens & Sprouting 61
   How to grow sprouts in a glass jar 65
   How to Grow Microgreens 67
Chapter 9: Raw Honey 69
   Honey-Basil Tea Recipe 73

Chapter 10: Houseplants 75
Chapter 11: Thought, Meditation & Prayer 81
    How to Meditate 86
Chapter 12: Exercise & Movement 89
    How to do Breath of Fire 94
Chapter 13: Natural Cleaning Products 97
    Shower Spray Recipe 102
Chapter 14: Skin Care Products 103
    Delightfully Divine Natural Deodorant 107
    Baby Gemz Vegan Handmade Soap bar 108
    Chocolate soap. 109
Resources 113
Author Biography 119

CHAPTER 1:
Nasal Irrigation Device

NASAL IRRIGATION IS a traditional Ayurvedic practice used to protect and soothe the respiratory tract. A nasal irrigation device, or "neti pot," is used to rinse the sinus cavities with a saline solution. Though it may sound like a strange and unusual practice, it is often recommended by Western physicians to relieve congestion and remove irritants. It uses no chemicals other than sea salt and can be a useful replacement for harsh decongestants.

Our nose is a gateway that protects us from intruders like allergens, pollution, bacteria, and viruses. It warms and moisturizes the air we breathe, filters out impurities, and helps the body detoxify. Rinsing the sinuses helps support all these important processes, as it can remove mucus and swelling so breathing is easier, lubricate nasal passages, soothe sinus headaches and pain, relieve a runny nose, prevent illness, and reduce the use of antihistamine medications.

Neti pots can be made from a variety of materials, from copper to plastic to ceramic. They also come in a variety of shapes but basically resemble a small teapot. You can find neti pots almost anywhere—drug stores, online, and health food stores.

While the process of irrigating the sinuses is quite simple, there are a few things that are **essential** to do correctly for your safety:

- Use sterile water. NEVER use water straight from the tap: tap water must be boiled for 3 to 5 minutes (and completely cooled). You could also use distilled water.

- Use a saline solution, NOT plain water. Make sure you use non-iodized salt and completely dissolve it, or it will sting and irritate your delicate sinuses. I recommend using Himalayan salt, but you can also buy special Neti pot salt that is finely ground and dissolves easily.

- Keep your hands and equipment as clean as possible

- Clean the pot with soap after each use. Be sure to rinse and clean it with sterile water. Dry it completely before storing.

- If you tend to have nosebleeds, you may want to talk to your doctor before using nasal irrigation or avoid the practice completely.

To rinse:

- You can use a pre-made saline solution, but it is easy to create your own. Just use a half-teaspoon of salt per cup of water. Slightly warm water can be very soothing but do not use hot water.

- Place the saline solution in the neti pot and tilt your head to the right over the sink.

- Gently pour the saline solution into your left nostril. It will flow through your sinus cavity and exit through the right nostril. (There are a number of videos on

Chapter 1: Nasal Irrigation Device

YouTube that demonstrate the proper use of the neti pot, which can be very helpful.)
- Repeat the process on the other side.
- Gently blow your nose after rinsing to remove all the liquid from your sinuses.
- Be sure to clean and dry your neti pot properly.

If the neti pot seems like too much of a challenge, you could try using a saline spray. There are many options available at drugstores, but I would recommend trying to find a natural one at a health food store, if possible. While it does not rinse away congestion or as many allergens, it does help soothe inflammation and, like the neti pot, is great for sore throats and irritated sinuses.

CHAPTER 2:
Essential Oils

WHILE PEOPLE WITH allergies may be particularly sensitive to certain scents, this should not deter you from utilizing the power of essential oils. Essential oils, when carefully chosen, offer healing not only with fragrance, but as botanical medicine. They can be found in many skin care and natural cleaning products, and used in aromatherapy and cooking. Soothing stress and relieving the discomfort of allergy systems helps strengthen and tone the body. A relaxing scent can also encourage you to breathe more deeply, which relaxes and helps strengthen the lungs.[3]

Essential oils are the highly concentrated natural oils of plants. It takes a tremendous amount of the plant to make even a small amount of oil. That is why many oils, such as rose, can be so expensive. The oils also contain the healing properties of that plant, in a very concentrated form.

Both physical illness and emotional concerns can be improved using essential oils, which is especially helpful when dealing with the discomfort of allergy symptoms. Allergy symptoms are often challenging and stressful, as anyone scrambling to find a tissue or trying not to rub itching eyes knows all too well. Oils can soothe the physical and emotional discomfort allergies create. The oils can be diluted and applied to the skin, or inhaled by using a diffuser.

Some excellent choices to consider when wrestling with allergies include:

- **Lavender**. The scent of this oil can reduce stress hormones in the blood, so it is commonly used for relaxation. It can be a useful anti-inflammatory, so diffusing it can help soothe irritated lungs and nasal passages. If you enjoy the scent, a few drops in an evening bath or on your pillow can help induce sleep.

- **Peppermint**. Peppermint is one of the few oils that can be taken internally. It is wonderful for digestive discomfort. It is also an expectorant, so can help clear out congestion and minimize the inflammation associated with allergies. Peppermint also stimulates mental alertness and clarity.

- **Frankincense**. This oil can be used for a variety of purposes, including relaxation, relieving stress, and healing insect bites and skin abrasions. Its scent is often used in spiritual ceremonies and can help with depression and auto-immune issues. It is very potent, so be careful not to overdo it.

- **Grapefruit & Lemon**. Lemon essential oil is a terrific detoxifier and can help heal acne spots. It is also stimulating and can help clear and sharpen your mind. Grapefruit has similar properties to lemon oil and can help with jet lag. Both citrus oils have antiseptic qualities and are often used in natural cleaning products. They are also helpful in soothing coughs, supporting the immune system, clearing congestion, and encouraging drainage. It can also help remove allergens from the air when diffused.

- **Eucalyptus**. If you have issues that affect your breathing, this may be your favorite essential oil. It

Chapter 2: Essential Oils

can help clear sinuses and congestion due to its strong scent and antibacterial properties. It is also great for sore muscles. Never ingest this oil or use it without diluting it; its strength can cause significant irritation. Mix a few drops with coconut oil and peppermint to create a wonderful vapor rub.

Please remember that essential oils are very powerful and could trigger further allergic reactions in sensitive individuals. When using essential oils, please be sure to consult a certified aroma therapist about using them safely. Since essential oils are absorbed into the body, it is important to use high-quality oils that are pure and from a reputable company. Most oils should never be applied on your skin undiluted; their strength could cause a reaction. You can dilute the essential oils with water to create a spray, or use a carrier oil to make a lotion. Generally, you should avoid ingesting essential oils. Essential oil use is not recommended for children under six months of age and pregnant women in the first trimester.

Essential Oil Recipes

Chapter 2: Essential Oils

Oil of Oregano Recipe
for immune boosting

Ingredients

Oregano Essential Oil

Extra Virgin Olive Oil

Directions

1. Fill a sterilized glass (amber or blue) 2-ounce dropper bottle with extra virgin olive oil.
2. Place 15 drops of oregano essential oil into the dropper bottle. Cap the bottle and shake vigorously.
3. Use two drops under the tongue and hold for 10 seconds.
4. Use twice a day, for a maximum of 14 days.

**If you are on medication, wait 3 hours before or after before taking this oil. The oil is best taken on an empty stomach.

Oregano is commonly used in this form for its antibacterial, antiviral and anti-inflammatory properties. Many professional singers use oil of oregano as a natural means of maintaining their voices for optimal performance.

Chapter 2: Essential Oils

RECIPE FOR DIGESTIVE HEALTH & RESPIRATORY SYSTEM

Ingredients

Peppermint essential oil

8 ounces of alkaline or filtered water

Directions

1. Put two drops of the essential oil into 8 ounces of water.
2. Drink on an empty stomach.

Peppermint essential oil is used to inhibit mucous secretions because it has a menthol component. It may also provide relief for blocked sinus passages. It is great for stomach and digestive ailments, such as flatulence, cramps and nausea, as it acts as a mild anesthetic for the stomach wall.

Recipe for the Skin

Ingredients

>Lavender essential oil

>Good quality plant-based oil (almond, hemp seed, olive, coconut oil, etc.)

Directions

1. Fill a clean 16-ounce bottle with the plant-base oil of your choice.
2. Put 10 drops of lavender essential oil in the bottle, seal and shake well.

This can be used as a body oil or as a replacement for lotion to moisturize the skin. It is best used after a bath or shower.

Lavender essential oil is known for its calming effects and helps with easing minor aches and pains. It can be used to soothe headaches caused by allergy symptoms.

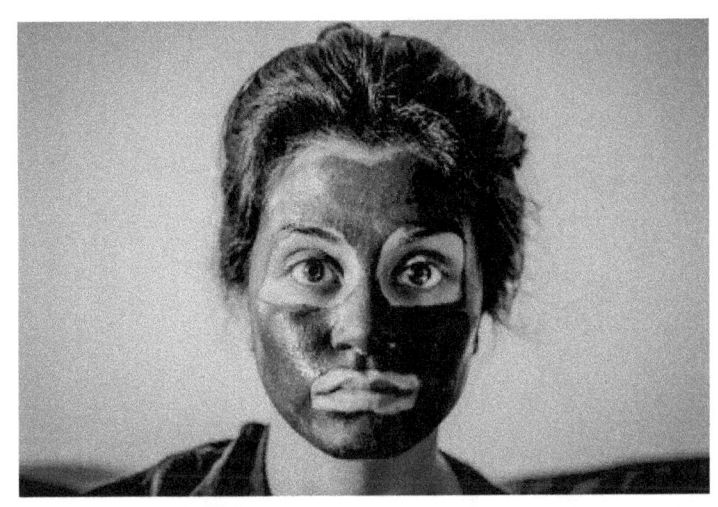

CHAPTER 3:
Bentonite Clay

Y̲OU MAY BE wondering, just what is bentonite clay? It is a dry, powdered clay made up of volcanic ash and named after the largest known clay deposit in Fort Benton, Montana. It is also known as "healing clay" or "montmorillonite."

This strong detoxifying properties can be helpful for allergy sufferers by removing toxins and allergens from the skin and body. This clay was used by our ancient ancestors around the world for centuries for its healing and detoxifying properties.[4] Bentonite clay has a strong electromagnetic charge and acts as a magnet in the body to attract and remove toxins. It can be used both internally and externally; reducing toxins can help support the immune system and reduce allergic symptoms.

When mixed with water, the clay swells, activating its magnetic properties. When it encounters toxins, heavy metals, or chemicals, it bonds with them, so they are removed from the body. As it draws out these toxins, it also deposits minerals. As a result, it balances out the pH level of the body by making it more alkaline. Bentonite clay has a high concentration of minerals, including silica, calcium, magnesium, iron and potassium. Most clays are either high in sodium or calcium. Clay that is high in sodium and low in calcium swells more than clay high in calcium.[5]

Sodium bentonite is one of the most common types used. This clay is used for detoxification externally and expands six times its initial size when mixed with water. It is frequently the main ingredient in many beauty products because it assists with balancing the pH of the skin. It is soothing for skin irritations and conditions such as acne or eczema. It can be a used in a bath or as a poultice.

Preliminary studies indicate that bentonite clay is able to absorb coronavirus, which causes the common cold and other respiratory tract illnesses.[6] It has also been shown to help heal bacterial infections, including antibiotic-resistant strains such as MRSA and Salmonella.[7] These properties can help support the immune system and reduce the toxic load on your body, which improves allergy symptoms and may help prevent an allergic reaction in the first place.

Calcium bentonite clay can be used internally and **must** be food grade quality. The best time of the day to consume the clay is in the morning on an empty stomach. It aids in re-mineralizing the body with calcium and silica. If you choose to use it internally, wait an hour before or after eating. Also, if you take medications or supplements, wait at least 2 hours, as the clay may absorb them before your body can metabolize them. If you are taking medications, it is a good idea to consult your doctor before taking bentonite clay internally.

When using bentonite clay, do not allow it to touch anything metal. Because of the clay's electromagnetic properties, metal will reduce its effectiveness. Use glass or plastic containers and utensils. Remember that bentonite clay is a mineral-rich substance and may contain lead. It is important to purchase it from a reliable and trustworthy source, such as Redmond Clay. The FDA has warned against using "Best Bentonite

Chapter 3: Bentonite Clay

Clay" from Guthrie, Oklahoma, and "Bentonite Me Baby" for personal care due to high levels of lead.[8]

Calcium Bentonite Clay Tonic Recipe

Ingredients

    1 teaspoon of calcium bentonite clay

    8 to 16 ounces of alkaline or filtered water

Directions

Stir one teaspoon of the calcium bentonite clay into 8 to 16 ounces of water and drink every other day. This will assist with detoxifying the body and balance your digestive system.

You can also use the clay as a mask or foot soak to remove toxins from the skin.

CHAPTER 4:
Water

WATER IS ESSENTIAL for life. A healthy adult can only live about a week without water. If our water levels drop, the body will protect essential organs and processes by pulling water from other areas, compromising their function. For example, just a two percent drop in water levels will cause your brain to shrink, leading to headaches and decreased concentration. [9]

Proper hydration is especially important for those individuals who suffer from allergies. Our immune system relies on water to keep individual cells functioning at peak efficiency. Water is also necessary to create immune system fluids that dilute and remove toxins.

Extended dehydration can actually make your allergies worse in several ways:

- When you are dehydrated, you may produce fewer antibodies that block allergic reactions. When there are fewer antibodies, your body will create more histamine in order to deal with allergens in an effort to protect itself. This results in allergy symptoms that are more frequent and intense.

- Long-term dehydration causes increased histamine production with symptoms similar to those caused by seasonal allergies.[10] Without adequate hydration, you will wind up dealing with histamines from your allergens, as well as histamines from lack of water—a double whammy!

- Finally, histamines control water flow in your body. If you are dehydrated and fighting allergens, your body will release even more histamines in an effort to get more water flowing to support your immune system. This results in a vicious cycle that worsens your allergic symptoms.

Supporting the immune system is essential when dealing with allergies. Dehydration inhibits the body's ability to fight off infection. Water is necessary for the removal of waste products through our digestive and elimination systems, including our skin. Constipation, kidney stones and urinary tract infections can occur when you are chronically dehydrated, and toxins build up as water is shunted away from the task of waste elimination. Our cells are also dependent upon proper hydration to perform their functions properly.

Every morning upon rising I drink at least 20 ounces (about 2.5 cups) of room temperature water. Done consistently, this practice has helped me flush toxins out of my body and improve my digestion. This is especially important while we sleep, when the body tends to cleanse and repair our cells.

When determining how much water you need, remember the old "eight glasses of water a day" advice is just a guideline, not a rule.[11] Exercise, a hot environment, sweating, caffeine or alcohol consumption (diuretics), increased stress and certain medications or supplements all may affect the water you need. Experiment to find the right amount for your body. Also, keep in mind that we get about 20 percent of our water from the

Chapter 4: Water

foods we eat, so fruits and vegetables are a good way to "eat" your water.

If you are not used to drinking water in the morning, just start off with a small quantity. By drinking water as soon as you wake up, you are restoring the water you lost during sleep and giving yourself an "internal shower."

Warm water, whether you drink it as a tea or with some lemon and honey, can be tremendously soothing for a sore throat, congestion, or general illness. Try varying the temperature of your water to see if you prefer warm, room temperature, or cold water. You can even infuse your water with fruits, vegetables, and herbs for flavor and added health benefits.

CITRUS INFUSED WATER RECIPE

This recipe tastes best when the ingredients are fresh, so drink it within a day or two.

Ingredients

    8 spearmint or peppermint leaves

    1 orange, cut into slices

    1 lemon, cut into slices

    1 liter of alkaline or filtered water

Directions

1. Place all the ingredients into a pitcher or mason jar.
2. Stir thoroughly.
3. Allow mixture to settle for about 5-6 hours at room temperature.
4. Place in the refrigerator and drink it within 24 hours

Chapter 4: Water

CUCUMBER MINT WATER

Cucumber water is a healthy and refreshing drink. The mint makes it a rejuvenating treat even on the hottest days. Mint can also help with congestion.

Ingredients

½ cucumber

1 liter of water

5 - 7 whole fresh mint leaves

Pinch of Pink Himalayan sea salt

Directions

1. Slice cucumber into 15 to 20 thin pieces.
2. Fill pitcher with water, mint, salt, and cucumber slices.

Tip: Use a wooden spoon to crush the mint leaves against the sides of the pitcher. It releases flavor and makes your water delicious!

Cucumber Lemon Water Recipe

Ingredients

- 1 to 2 peeled or unpeeled cucumbers
- 1 liter of water
- 1 to 2 lemons

Directions

1. Slice cucumber into ½-inch slices.
2. Juice the lemons.
3. Fill pitcher with water, lemon juice and cucumber slices.
4. Let it sit for an hour or overnight in the refrigerator.

This mixture should last about three days in the refrigerator.

Chapter 4: Water

Watermelon Citrus Water

Ingredients

1 cup of fresh watermelon

Juice of ½ lemon

Juice of ½ orange

1 lemon wedge

1 orange wedge

5 - 8 slices of cucumber

1 liter of water

Directions

1. Place all the ingredients into a pitcher.
2. Stir and refrigerate.

The addition of cucumber helps soften the citrus flavor.

Oregano Rosemary Watermelon Infused Water

Adding herbs like rosemary and oregano to a fruity drink may seem strange, but the flavor is complex and tasty. The strong flavors of the herbs compliment the sweetness of fruits like watermelon.

Ingredients

1 ½ - 2 stems fresh rosemary

1 ½ - 2 stems fresh oregano (or 1 tsp. dried)

½ cucumber, thinly sliced

1 cup of watermelon

Directions

1. Bring about 4 cups of water to a rolling boil.
2. Remove from heat and place the rosemary and oregano in the water. Let the herbs infuse in the water for 15-20 minutes. Let it cool.
3. Blend or juice the watermelon. Mix with the water and cucumbers.
4. Let this mixture sit in the refrigerator for about 1 hour.

CHAPTER 5:
Probiotic & Fermented Foods

THE IDEA OF fermenting food and purposefully ingesting bacteria may sound counter-intuitive or even unpleasant at first. However, probiotics and fermented foods can be an important resource for combating allergies of all types. This is because a strong immune system is dependent upon robust gut health.

About 70% or more of your immune system resides in your gut. Your gut contains over 500 types of bacteria or "gut flora." Several studies indicate that adequate numbers of these beneficial bacteria in the gut reduces the occurrence and severity of allergies.[12] These bacteria are necessary for us to digest our food and absorb nutrients and they also enhance our immune system and protect us from pathogenic bacteria. Ingesting fermented foods or probiotics replenishes our supply of good bacteria so they outnumber the bad and can help manage allergies.

Fermented foods go through a process called lacto fermentation, where naturally occurring bacteria digest the sugar and starch in the food, creating lactic acid. As a by-product, this process creates B-vitamins, Omega-3 fatty acids, and a variety of healthful enzymes and probiotics (healthful bacteria).

Many studies indicate that consuming fermented and probiotic foods improve overall allergy symptoms. For instance, one study found that probiotics can improve "allergic rhinitis," or runny nose.[13] Another study found that individuals who took a probiotic supplement experienced less discomfort and fewer allergy symptoms generally than those that took a placebo.[14]

Antibiotics can kill off good bacteria, allowing opportunistic strains to multiply. Stress, birth control pills, and pollutants can compromise healthy gut bacteria. A diet heavy in refined carbohydrates and sugars feeds pathogenic bacteria and yeasts, such as candida. To support the good bacteria in your gut, it is helpful to think about starving the pathogenic bacteria and continually replenishing probiotic bacteria. For those with compromised immunity or digestion, taking a supplemental probiotic capsule may also be helpful. However, it is still important to eat fermented foods for the diversity of organisms needed by our bodies.

Examples of fermented foods include yogurt and kefir (including those made with coconut), fermented vegetables such as sauerkraut and kimchi, miso (fermented soybean paste often used in soups), kombucha, and rejuvelac. Remember that for probiotic bacteria to support your health, they must be alive when ingested. Just keep in mind that if something has been pasteurized, or exposed to heat, it will not contain active probiotics.

It is easy to make your own sauerkraut, fermented vegetables, or puddings at home. If you'd like to purchase these foods at the store, they will be in the refrigerated section. Bubbie's is a good brand of living sauerkraut and pickles. Fermented foods are enjoying increased popularity at present, so you can find a wide variety of pickled vegetables, kombucha and cultured yogurt at most health food and grocery stores.

Chapter 5: Probiotic & Fermented Foods

Keep in mind that you want to start out by slowly introducing fermented foods and probiotic supplements. They can create a cleansing reaction as good bacteria crowd out the bad. When the bad bacteria die off, they release toxins that can make you feel very ill, even though what is happening is healthy. It is best to go slowly and introduce foods a little at a time to see how your body feels. Soon you will find you begin to crave these nourishing foods and your digestion and immune system will strengthen.

Fermented Chia Pudding Recipe

Ingredients

- 1 cup of plant-based milk (almond, coconut, hemp)
- 2 teaspoons of chia seeds
- 1 probiotic capsule

Directions

1. Open the probiotic capsule and empty it into a mason jar.
2. Mix in the chia seeds and plant-based milk.
3. Cover with a dish towel and keep it on your counter overnight. Once it is finished, it can be stored, covered, in the refrigerator.
4. If you want to add flavorings such as honey or fruit, add them just before you eat the pudding, so they don't affect the probiotics.

Chapter 5: Probiotic & Fermented Foods

Rejuvelac Recipe

Rejuvelac is a nutritious probiotic drink developed by raw food pioneer Ann Wigmore. While it is traditionally made with wheat berries, those who are gluten-sensitive can use gluten-free grains such as quinoa.

Ingredients

1 cup of soft wheat berries, rye, quinoa, or buckwheat

Directions

1. Place the wheat berries (or grains of your choice) in a mason jar with a screen top and fill with water.
2. Soak the grain for 24 hours. Drain off water, leaving the grain in jar. Rinse once or twice a day until little sprout tails appear.
3. Place sprouted grain in large jar with a top that allows air to circulate. Add 4 cups of water and let sit on your counter for 2-3 days.

4. Watch for the water to get cloudy and little bubbles begin to form.
5. Taste...it should taste clean and fresh with a hint of lemon. Strain the liquid (rejuvelac) and store it in covered glass container in the refrigerator. It will keep for at least a week—just make sure it continues to smell and taste fresh. You can reuse your grain of choice to make a second batch.

Tip: If you don't wish to use the sprouted grain, it is a wonderful addition to compost.

CHAPTER 6:
Nuts & Seeds

THE POWER OF nuts and seeds extends far beyond the humble peanut butter and jelly sandwich. A wonderful and satiating snack, they are concentrated sources of healthy monounsaturated fats, protein, vitamin E, minerals, and antioxidants. This high-powered nutrition can strengthen your immune system, leading to fewer allergic symptoms.

For the greatest nutritional benefit, nuts should usually be eaten raw. However, even roasted they are still good sources of nutrients. Many of your favorite nuts also confer specific health benefits. For example, walnuts can help reduce the risk of some cancers and improve brain health. Brazil nuts are a great source of selenium; you should not eat more than a couple of these nuts every day because they are such a potent source of this mineral.

Sometimes it is difficult to tell the difference between a nut and a seed. Almonds are seeds, though we often think of them as nuts; they are a great source of biotin, a B vitamin that helps manage blood sugar. Sunflower seeds can prevent migraines, soothe anxiety, protect against heart disease, high blood pressure, and arthritis pain.

Some nuts and seeds you might wish to sample include:

- **Almonds**. Almonds assist the body in absorbing fat-soluble nutrients, such as vitamins A and E. These nutrients are essential for a strong immune system. They also help balance the pH of your body and aid digestion, both of which improves immunity. Almonds contain high levels of antioxidants, which are concentrated in the brown skin. They are low in carbs, but high in protein, healthy fats and fiber, making them a great choice for diabetics. Most people are deficient in magnesium and a two-ounce serving of almonds provides half the RDA of this important mineral. Some studies indicate that magnesium is helpful in balancing blood sugar.[15]

- **Cashews**. Sometimes struggling with allergies and their symptoms can drain you emotionally, as well as physically. Cashews are a good source of iron, magnesium, Vitamin B6, protein, amino acids and omega-3 fats. They can improve your mood and may even help with mild depression.

- **Chia seeds**. Chia is an ancient crop, sacred to the Aztecs and one of the staples of their diet as early as 3500 BC. They contain vitamin C, protein and iron, along with fiber and omega-3 fatty acids. Chia also contains compounds that alleviate joint pain and reduce depression. These remarkable seeds can absorb almost 10 times their weight in liquid. Because of this, they are filling and soothing to the digestive tract. It is important to combine these with liquid before consuming them. When combined with liquid, such as almond or coconut milk, they create a pudding that is similar in texture to tapioca pudding. They can also be ground into a powder and added to

Chapter 6: Nuts & Seeds

foods, but it is best to do this right before consuming so their oils don't become rancid.

- **Pumpkin seeds**. Also known as "pepitas," these green seeds have a soft, chewy texture and delicate taste. They contain vitamins B, C, E and K, as well as a variety of minerals, fiber, and omega-3 fatty acids. They also contain a number of phytosterols that support health, and have a low fat content compared to other nuts and seeds. They can support your immune system, lower cholesterol, stabilize blood sugar, improve depression and anxiety, support prostate and heart health, and protect against some types of cancer. They are also wonderful for the eyes, hair, and skin. They make a great snack and, because they are soft, are easily blended into smoothies, soups, or nut butter. Added to salads or baked goods, they provide a nice texture.

- **Flaxseeds**. These brown or gold seeds contain alpha-linolenic acid, fiber, and lignans. They are also high in B vitamins and various minerals. Because they become mucilaginous when soaked in water, they support regular bowels movements and help you feel full. Skin and hair benefit from their oils, and they also help improve PMS, reduce cholesterol and cancer risks, and stabilize blood sugar. Whole flaxseeds make healthy crackers; when ground they make a tasty porridge or can be included in baking. Since they do absorb a good deal of water, be sure to stay hydrated when consuming them. Pregnant and breast-feeding women, and those who take blood thinners, should avoid flaxseeds due to the phytoestrogens the seeds contain.

Nuts and seeds offer tremendous nutrition, but they are also common allergens. Be sure you are not allergic to them before adding them to your diet. They are also very concentrated sources of nutrients and fat, so eating them in moderation still conveys health benefits. The oils in these foods can easily go rancid, so be sure to store them in airtight containers.

Chapter 6: Nuts & Seeds

Basic Nut & Seed Milk Recipe

Ingredients

1 cup of raw nuts of your choice (If you have a nut allergy then substitute raw seeds in place of nuts such as sunflower, pepitas, or hemp seeds.)

4 cups of alkaline or filtered water

2 Medjool Dates (optional)

1 tsp of Vanilla Extract (optional)

Directions

1. Soak the nuts in 2-3 cups water for at least eight hours or overnight.
2. Drain and discard water.

3. Blend soaked nuts or seeds with 4 cups fresh water, medjool dates, and vanilla extract until almost smooth.
4. Strain the blended nut mixture using muslin, a nut milk bag, or clean nylon stocking.
5. Refrigerate. The milk will keep in the refrigerator for 3-4 days.

CHAPTER 7:
Spices & Herbs

SPICES AND HERBS give our food depth and flavor, but did you know they can also help manage allergies? Herbs and spices were historically used as medicines, long before they were incorporated into meal preparation. The wonderful thing about this type of medicine is that it actually tastes good!

Most of us use herbs and spices every day, but never think much about them beyond the flavor they impart. Herbs and spices come from various parts of a dazzling array of plants and, in addition to their scents and tastes, contain compounds that can benefit our bodies. You may be surprised to discover how your favorite spices have been supporting your health while you enjoy your food.

Some herbs and spices that are particularly helpful in managing allergies include:

- **Butterbur.** This perennial shrub was shown in a study to be as effective as an antihistamine in managing hay fever and grass allergy symptoms.[16] It helped relieve symptoms such as sneezing, runny nose, congestion, itching, and watering eyes in five days. Butterbur is less likely to cause drowsiness or the other side effects of antihistamines.

It is generally not recommended for children, those over 65, or those with allergies to plants such as daisies or ragweed. Butterbur also contains pyrrolizidine alkaloids (Pas) which can damage the liver; and butterbur preparation you ingest should be labeled "PA-free."

- **Garlic**. Garlic is a member of the onion family. Garlic has been used medicinally throughout history. The compound that gives garlic its familiar pungent scent is also its active ingredient, allicin. Garlic supports the immune system and can be helpful for preventing or speeding healing from the common cold.[17] It also can benefit heart health by reducing cholesterol and high blood pressure.[18]

- **Turmeric**. Turmeric is a root that you can purchase in powder form or fresh from the produce area. You have probably seen turmeric as the bright yellow component of some curries, or perhaps in "golden milk," a popular coconut milk beverage. Turmeric contains curcumin, which is a powerful antioxidant.[19] Curcumin is difficult for the body to absorb; it is best to take turmeric with piperine (contained in black pepper). This combination increases absorption by almost 2,000%.

Turmeric has been used in Ayurvedic medicine to treat all sorts of inflammatory conditions, including sinus issues.[20] Inflammation has been cited as the precursor to almost every sort of disease, and is a major component of allergic reactions. Curcumin fights damage from free radicals which cause disease and cause our body to age prematurely.

- **Ginger.** Ginger is a root like turmeric, with a spicy, sweet flavor. Ginger is excellent from treating nausea from chemotherapy, morning sickness, sea sickness and other causes. It is an anti-inflammatory and can also help manage pain. An interesting study showed that ginger and cinnamon mixed in sesame oil and applied topically helped pain and stiffness as well as aspirin or ibuprofen.[21] It is pungent and can help clear sinuses.

- **Parsley**. Parsley contains vitamins A and C. It has anti-inflammatory properties and may inhibit the production of histamines. Keep in mind that parsley is a diuretic, so be sure to talk with your doctor before taking supplements or consuming large quantities of it. This is especially true if you are taking medication, as it might flush it out of your body before it has a chance to work.

- **Reishi Mushrooms**. Reishi can reduce the production of histamine and improve oxygen delivery to the body. It is relaxing, anti-inflammatory, and supports the immune system.[22] It is usually ground into a powder and makes a coffee-like drink when mixed with plant-based milks or in smoothies.

- **Mullein**. The leaves and flowers of this herb are usually prepared as a tea to nourish the respiratory tract. Traditionally, it is used for relief of dry coughs and allergies. It encourages the removal of mucus and soothes irritated mucous membranes. It supports the lymph glands which helps boost immunity.

- **Black seed**. Otherwise known as Nigella sativa, black seeds are full of antioxidants and can provide allergy relief. They were used in ancient times for every sort of illness. Topical application of the oil to the sinuses provided some improvement to allergic rhinitis.[23] The oil can also be taken internally as a supplement. It has anti-inflammatory properties that help reduce congestion and itching.

Chapter 7: Spices & Herbs

Apple Ginger Juice Recipe

Ingredients

1 medium apple, cut in slices
½ tbsp. grated ginger

Directions

1. Juice or blend both ingredients.
2. Serve immediately for best results.

GOLDEN MILK RECIPE

Ingredients

1 cup (8 ounces) plant-based milk

½ tsp ground turmeric

¼ tsp ground cinnamon

1 tsp grated ginger root or ¼ tsp ginger powder

Ground black pepper or black seed powder to taste

Natural sweetener to taste (Raw honey, pure maple syrup, or stevia)

Cayenne to taste (optional)

Directions

1. In a saucepan, add milk of choice, turmeric, ginger, cinnamon, and black pepper or black seed powder.
2. Whisk to combine and warm over medium heat. Heat until hot to the touch but not boiling - about 4 minutes - whisking frequently.

3. Turn off heat and taste to adjust flavor. Add sweetener to taste, or more turmeric or ginger for intense spice and flavor.
4. Serve immediately. Best when fresh, though leftovers can be stored covered in the refrigerator for 2-3 days. Reheat on the stovetop for best results.

CHAPTER 8:
Microgreens & Sprouting

MICROGREENS AND SPROUTS are tiny but mighty! These nutritional powerhouses provide a wealth of protein, vitamins, minerals, and enzymes in a small package. The difference between sprouts and microgreens is simply the growth-stage of the plant. Sprouts are the just-germinated seeds and microgreens are plants with their very first leaves.

Sprouts and microgreens are economical and fun to grow at home with simple equipment. While almost any vegetable seed can be sprouted, their nutritional offerings and flavors differ. Some types of vegetable seeds even provide additional support for allergy sufferers.

For instance, sunflower, broccoli and radish sprouts and microgreens are good decongestants, clearing and nourishing the lungs. Basil can help build your immune system. Broccoli sprouts contain sulforaphane, which fights cancer.[24] (These do have a strong sulfur smell when sprouting.) Alfalfa sprouts are a salad bar mainstay due to their mild taste and high amounts of vitamins B, C, and K. They also help reduce cholesterol. Do NOT sprout red kidney beans, as they become toxic when sprouted. Kidney beans must always be cooked before eating.

Keep in mind that the humid environment that sprouts the seeds can also support the growth of bacteria. There have been reports that bacteria present on the seed can cause it to grow.[25] Keeping your sprouting equipment clean and rinsing the sprouts regularly is important. If you are still concerned, you can try soaking the sprouts in lemon juice diluted with water for 15 minutes, as that may help kill any bacteria.

Chapter 8: Microgreens & Sprouting

How to grow sprouts in a glass jar

Choose a jar. The easiest way to grow sprouts is a simple glass jar that is large enough to hold the sprouts. If you can find one that has a wide mouth, like a mason jar, that is ideal.

- **Sterilize the jar.** Wash the jar with very hot, soapy water. Rinse well and dry. Be sure to keep your hands and utensils clean when gardening with your sprouts.

- **Choose a seed.** If you are sprouting very small seeds, you might want to use a lid that has mesh on it. If you are sprouting larger seeds, like grains, you'll want a half-gallon jar.

- **Rinse the seeds.** Always use cool water. Check for any small rocks or other matter.

- **Soak the seeds.** Fill the jar about ¾ full with water. Cover with a mesh lid or cloth and put a rubber band around the mouth of the jar. Soak until seeds double in size—about eight hours for most seeds. The time needed will vary according to the seed and temperature; warmer temperatures require less time.

- **Drain the seeds.** It is very important to drain them for several hours and allow air circulation. Mesh lids are convenient here, as you can prop the jar in a dishrack at an angle and let it sit.

- **Continue to rinse and drain**. You'll need to repeat at least 3 times a day for about 2-3 days. If temperatures are warm, rinse more often.
- **Final rinse**. When the seeds have grown enough and are ready to eat, rinse and drain one final time. Sprouts can be stored in the refrigerator wrapped in a paper towel or dishcloth.

Chapter 8: Microgreens & Sprouting

How to Grow Microgreens

Microgreens provide the same benefits as sprouts, but since they are grown in soil they don't have the same risks from bacteria. Lettuce, all types of greens, mustard, and daikon radish are flavorful choices. Microgreens are four to six times more nutritious than the mature plant.

Equipment needed:

- A low tray with a cover
- Light soil, such as potting soil
- Seeds

To grow your microgreens:

- **Place soil in tray**. You'll need about half an inch of soil in the tray.
- **Water the soil**. Don't let it get soggy or water-logged. If it's too wet, drain the water.
- **Rinse the seeds**. Check for debris and remove any stones.
- **Put seeds in soil**. Spread them evenly over the soil.

- **Mist the seeds.** This is easiest with a spray bottle.
- **Cover the tray.** Avoid direct sunlight, as this will dry the seeds out.
- **Water daily.** This is easiest with a spray bottle at first. Once the seeds sprout, it is better to pour water in so the leaves don't get wet. Drain the water if there's too much.
- **Time to harvest.** When the first green leaves appear, you can eat the microgreens. If you wish, you can continue to water and grow the greens until the second pair of leaves appears. To harvest the sprouts, cut them just above the soil.

Microgreens do not store very well, but they will keep a few days in the refrigerator in a covered container if you dry them with paper towels. If you'd like to purchase a specialized sprouter jar or mesh lids, there are many sources on the internet. A good resource is the Cultures for Health website (www.culturesforhealth.com). They have reasonably-priced sprouting seeds, kits, and lots of free recipes and information about sprouting, fermentation, and other do-it-yourself health foods.

CHAPTER 9:
Raw Honey

WINNIE-THE-POOH WAS DEFINITELY on to something in his endless pursuit of honey. While Pooh was right about the delicious flavor, honey can also be a wonderful resource for seasonal allergy sufferers. Honey has always been an important part of traditional medicine, used by the ancient Egyptians and other cultures to heal wounds, liver, heart and gastrointestinal problems.[26]

While there are few scientific studies that support the use of honey for healing allergies, there is a tremendous amount of anecdotal evidence.[27] I use raw, local honey in the spring and fall to control seasonal allergies; I take ½ teaspoon every morning a month before the height of the allergy season. I personally use honey pollinated by spring flowers for springtime allergies and then switch to fall-pollinated honey for the autumn months.

The idea of honey improving seasonal allergies works the same way allergy shots do. That is, you receive a small dose of the allergen over time and your body becomes desensitized to it. Since honey contains small amounts of pollen, consuming it over time might work the way immunotherapy, or allergy shots, do. Keep in mind that the honey will only contain the pollens that are collected by the bees, which are mostly from flowers. Many of the pollens that cause seasonal allergies, such as those from grass and trees, will likely only be present in small amounts, if at all. One study did indicate this might be effective by showing that overall allergy symptoms were fewer and less severe in the group that used raw honey.[28]

Regardless of whether you use honey to try to desensitize a pollen allergy, it can definitely be helpful in other ways. For instance, a spoonful of honey can work as a cough suppressant to help soothe a sore throat and dry cough. Some say the antioxidants, beneficial enzymes, vitamins, and minerals it contains can help fight viruses and bacteria and deeply nourish the body. It also makes a wonderful, moisturizing mask for the skin.

Cautionary Notes

- NEVER give honey in any form to children under 1 year old. Raw honey, in rare instances, may contain botulism spores. While this is not a problem for adults, babies do not have sufficiently developed immune systems to handle the toxin, which can lead to extreme illness or death.

- If you have allergies, it is best to consult with your doctor before consuming any honey. Honey has a great deal of fructose, so may not be a good choice for diabetics, those with blood sugar challenges, or people who are choosing to lose weight.

- Always use raw, unfiltered, local honey. At the very least, choose a honey that is from the same geographical region that you live; it is likely the same types of pollen will be in both locations. If in doubt, choose a wildflower honey, as it is likely to have some of the pollens that are causing your allergies. Choose honey that is free from chemicals and pesticides.

Chapter 9: Raw Honey

HONEY-BASIL TEA RECIPE

Ingredients

2 teaspoons of fresh or powdered ginger

1 liter of water

2 teaspoons of freshly squeezed lemon juice

2 tablespoon of raw Honey

10 Basil leaves

Directions

1. Bring water to a rolling boil, then turn off the heat.
2. Add ginger, lemon juice, and basil leaves. Steep for about 15 minutes.
3. Add raw honey and stir well.
4. For best results, serve warm. You may wish to keep it in a thermos so it stays warm longer.

Drink the tea throughout the day.

CHAPTER 10:
Houseplants

When pollen counts are at their highest, allergy sufferers often seek refuge indoors. Today's modern constructions are more energy-efficient than in the past, but can concentrate off-gassing chemicals from paint, carpet, and furniture in the air. While you can always purchase an air purifier, a more natural and beautiful way to ensure you have clean air is to fill your living space with houseplants.

In 1989, NASA put out a Clean Air Study that documents how plants are effective air purifiers; while it was meant for space flights, it is also applicable to the air in our homes.[29] When we exhale, we release carbon dioxide as waste and plants are able to convert this into oxygen. Plants are also able to absorb and neutralize harmful chemicals from the air, such as formaldehyde and benzene.

There are a tremendous variety of plants that will happily grow in a variety of environments. You may want to consider adding a few of the following easy-care plants to your home:

- **Snake plant or Mother-in-Law's Tongue.** This plant is known as "the bedroom plant" because it gives off oxygen during the night; other plants tend to take in oxygen at night. It filters formaldehyde, trichloroethylene, xylene, toluene, and benzene from the air. It is said to be able to thrive in a closet, as its light requirements are so low. It prefers less water or it will rot.

- **Cast iron plant.** This plant gets its name from its low maintenance requirements. It cannot tolerate direct sun, which may burn its leaves.

- **Pothos**. This vine comes in a huge variety of colors and patterns. Keep in mind that while it will survive in low light conditions, it needs medium sunlight to maintain the variegation in the leaves. It only wants water every seven to ten days; if you are heavy handed with water, the plant will rot.

- **Swiss Cheese Plant or Philodendron monstera**. This plant does best in bright, but not direct sunlight; an east-facing window is preferred. Try to avoid keeping it in a southern exposure, as it may burn the leaves. It requires adequate drainage, so be sure your pot has drainage holes and you keep a dish underneath to collect any drained water. It likes to dry out in between watering. The large leaves can collect dust, so allergy sufferers should make sure to wipe the plant with a damp towel occasionally. It is believed that the holes in the plant's leaves help make it more effective at getting sunlight in the rainforest.[30]

- **Dracaena.** This houseplant is great at removing benzene that comes from cigarette smoke, as well as formaldehyde, xylene and trichloroethylene. It does well with very infrequent watering. If you prefer a tall, thin plant for a room where you do not have a lot of floor space, this is a good option.

- **Spider plant.** These plants have long thin leaves that are usually striped with green and white. They work as both a potted or hanging plant. This plant is the highest performing in terms of toxin removal from the air. It is easy to care for and very hardy. They tolerate most conditions, but do like to have a bit of sunlight.

- **Peace lilies.** One of the most popular houseplants in the U.S., this evergreen does not require much light or water, but it does like a warm temperature and indirect light. It is good for reducing benzene, formaldehyde, and trichloroethylene. This plant can reduce mold in the air, as it absorbs mold spores and converts them into nutrients for itself.

Good plants choices for a bedroom, as well as other rooms, include:

- **Areca palm**. This plant is tall and can be placed in a corner. It removes formaldehyde, xylene, carbon monoxide, and toluene. It can also humidify a room in the winter because it releases moisture as it transpires (the process of the plant "breathing"). This plant is tropical, so it does require a fair amount of water and likes medium sunlight, such as indirect southern exposure. They grow quickly and can reach up to seven feet tall.

- **Boston fern.** This plant is another good choice for adding moisture to the air and removing formaldehyde. They are a bit difficult to grow, as they require ample sunlight and need to be misted regularly. If you have a bit of a green thumb, they are gorgeous plants.

- **Aloe vera.** Most people know aloe as a soothing gel for sunburns. Aloe is a succulent, so it requires very little water or care. It is a great plant for beginners and are good for children to grow. They grow slowly and adapt to a variety of light conditions; they do, however, need some amount of sunlight.

- Plants that do well with humidity or in a bathroom include:
- **Bromeliad or Air plant.** These are small, so do not pack the same air filtering power that larger plants may. However, they are unusual, adorable, and easy-care. They do not require soil and can hang from a string or placed in a glass holder. They absorb the humidity from showers and thus do not need watering. They also may reduce mold growth.
- **Chinese evergreen.** This plant grows best in low light with minimal watering—just every few weeks. It likes a warm, humid environment.

Keep in mind that though houseplants are wonderful air purifiers, many of them can be toxic if ingested. If you have children or pets,

Plants that are toxic to children and pets include Pothos, Peace Lily, Snake Plant or Mother-in-Law's Tongue, Swiss Cheese Plant or Philodendron, and more. Often the bitter taste of these plants will stop a pet or child from ingesting the large amount needed to create a problem, but it is best to do your research and choose plants that are best for your individual situation.

CHAPTER 11:
Thought, Meditation & Prayer

To achieve truly vibrant holistic health, we have to nourish the trinity of body, mind, and spirit. When we think of health, we often focus solely on our physical selves, because that is easy to see and feel. We often learn to ignore our needs of our heart, mind, and soul, such as love, community, and connection.

Your mind and spirit can heal, as well as create, disease in your physical body. Scientific studies have shown that positive thought processes, prayer, and meditation all can contribute meaningfully to an individual's health and well-being. Take some time to explore some of the practices offered below; you may be surprised at the difference they make to your health. They can all be customized so that they feel good to you and honor your individual beliefs and preferences.

Nourishing Your Thought Processes

- Observe how you talk to yourself. If you find negative thought patterns, don't judge yourself. Just observe—the goal here is simply to become aware, without criticism. Over time, you will start to see patterns and rhythms in your thought processes, assumptions, and conclusions. This provides a basis for letting go of beliefs that no longer serve you.

- Affirmations can be productive ways to introduce healthy thought patterns. For instance, you may wish to feel more loving towards yourself, so you might choose an affirmation such as "I completely and deeply love myself." Repeat it to yourself many times every day; it is best to say it out loud, looking at yourself in a mirror. If saying the affirmation to yourself creates a strong negative or disbelieving response, you'll want to revise it. For instance, you might use "I'm willing to learn to love myself," instead.

- Sometimes the support and guidance of another person can be helpful for healing. My free video series, Dropping Gemz™, offers short coaching sessions that talk about how to explore and heal destructive thought patterns.[31] Some of the topics covered include gratitude, letting go, forgiveness, and patience.

MEDITATION

There are many types of meditation, but they all aim to train your mind and reduce stress. The idea is to stop getting lost in all the "stories" and judgments our mind creates, so we gain more perspective and peace. Meditation benefits the nervous system in many ways, such as lowering blood pressure and heart rate and anxiety.

The most basic meditation, which is excellent for beginners and experts alike, is to simply observe the breath. You could also choose to repeat a word or mantra, watch a candle flame, or counting beads on a necklace. There are meditations that involve movement, such as tai chi, qigong, and walking meditation. Many martial arts involve meditation as well.

Mindfulness meditation has been shown to affect genes that control inflammation, which reduces stress, can relieve chronic back pain, and improve immunity.[32] Meditation is powerful, but requires regular practice to be effective; consistency will slowly strengthen your body and spirit.

Prayer

There are many spiritual practices that help us cope with and relieve stress, including the stress of allergies. Stress can be a trigger for many illnesses such as depression, high blood pressure, ulcers, and migraines. Spiritual practices, regardless of the tradition, can provide support and give us courage to stay proactive, even when life is painful and overwhelming. A spiritual practice can open your heart to your own sacredness and value, which can provide you with peace and support.

One study asked participants to meditate on a variety of mantras, such as "God is love," "I feel happy," and "Grass is green." Those that used the spiritual mantra had fewer headaches and better pain tolerance than those that used non-spiritual statements.[33]

Both prayer and meditation can slow your heart rate, reduce blood pressure, and increase theta waves in the brain.[34] This gives a sense of empowerment, alertness, and peace of mind. Prayer and meditation can increase levels of dopamine, which increases feelings of calm and happiness.

How to Meditate

1. Find a quiet place where you won't be disturbed.
2. Sit in a comfortable chair. You may also lie down.
3. Close your eyes.
4. Notice your breath. Do not try to change it, just observe.
5. Pay attention to the rise and fall of your chest and stomach, your inhale and exhale.
6. Observe your body. When your mind wanders, and it certainly will, just gently bring it back to your chosen focus. Don't worry or get frustrated, the point to just to observe, notice and refocus, even if you do it 100 times in the space of a few minutes. Over time, your ability to focus will strengthen.
7. Just like exercise for our bodies, we can get "sore muscles" if we do too much too soon. Do this for two to three minutes in the beginning, and gradually increase the time. If you find it is too relaxing and you fall asleep, you may wish to remain sitting or have your eyes open for the practice.

Chapter 11: Thought, Meditation & Prayer

Often when experiencing allergic symptoms, we experience congestion, a runny nose and sore throat. During these times, it may be extremely challenging to meditate on the breath. If this occurs, simply move your attention to another part of your body that is not related to your allergies, such as your hand, and focus on feeling any sensations that might be there.[35]

CHAPTER 12:
Exercise & Movement

WE'VE ALL HEARD that "sitting is the new smoking."[36] To make matters worse, studies indicate that even if you exercise strenuously for an hour every day, it isn't enough to prevent health issues from sitting the rest of the day. Most of us are already pressed for time and have sedentary jobs, so what are we to do? And when seasonal allergies strike, the last thing anyone wants to think about is going for a run. The key isn't to exercise harder and longer, it is simply to incorporate more movement into our daily lives.

Working out at the gym definitely provides health benefits, such as increased strength, stress release, and endurance. Sweating is detoxifying and cleansing. Our lymph system is completely dependent on our movement to function properly. Our bones and digestive system also require our bodies to move in order to remain strong and function properly.

Deep breathing helps clear and strengthen your lungs. Exercise also warms the body and supports the immune system. Gentle exercise can help the body expel congestion and toxins from allergens. In fact, one study did show that a short run can actually improve "allergic rhinitis" or runny nose.[37]

Keep in mind that the gym isn't the only option when it comes to adding more movement into our days. Think about the percentage of your day that you are actively engaged in movement. If you exercise an hour, and sit the rest of the day, your "motion quotient" is low. But if you walk to work, move throughout the day, pick up and play with your children, walk the dog, park far away, garden, and play sports, your "motion quotient" is high. This perspective allows you to get creative about how to add small, but consequential, movement into your existing schedule.

Some ideas to get more movement into your day could include:

- Sit on the floor, or use a meditation cushion. Change chairs or sit cross-legged in your chair. Think about purchasing a "wiggle cushion," which is an inexpensive inflated disk that allows you to move as you're sitting in a chair.

- Carry things. Park farther away and walk to the door carrying your bag or your groceries. Pick up your children or a stack of books. This helps engage different muscles than you might otherwise use.

- Take more walks. Walk instead of drive. Hiking through nature reconnects us to the earth. You can walk halls in an office building or a mall. Take the stairs or choose the furthest parking space.

- Reach, bend, squat. Stretch for things on the higher shelves and squat for things on the lower ones. Be careful to know your limits and use proper form—there should be no tension or pain.

- Lose your shoes. Going barefoot will exercise your feet. In fact, the more textured surfaces you can walk over, the better. Keep in mind if you always wear shoes, this may be a bit painful at first. Like everything

Chapter 12: Exercise & Movement

else, start small and work your way up. This stretches your feet, toes, and calves.

- At work, set a timer so you remember to take breaks. Walk to the restroom, bring a file to a colleague, or take lunch outside if you're able. Set up a short 15-minute stretching break with colleagues; many businesses encourage employees to look after their health and support these activities.

Keep in mind that activities you love, like dancing, any sort of sport, even table tennis, can get you moving and sweating. You may wish to explore gentle exercise options like Pilates, yoga, Feldenkrais, and rebounding.

The internet can be a great free resource for exercise and movement ideas. There are even many videos that demonstrate how to do all kinds of exercise, from yoga to weight lifting, taught by instructors with diverse body types and fitness levels. They can be an easy way to stay interested in exercise can support you in your fitness journey. Katy Bowman, a biomechanist, offers many wonderful books, DVDs, and free resources on her website that can help you incorporate more movement into your day.[38]

Gentle exercise that is incorporated into your day is easier to manage when dealing with allergic symptoms and, over time, can strengthen your body, reduce stress, and improve your immune response so that your allergy symptoms decrease or disappear.

How to do Breath of Fire

It takes time and practice to build up to the full breath of fire. If you are a beginner, start slowly and only practice for sessions of 30 seconds or less. This is a very cleansing pranayama (breath yoga) that, over time, can strengthen your lungs and reduce allergic symptoms.

1. Find a quiet place where you won't be disturbed.
2. Sit up either in a straight-backed chair or on the floor.
3. Lower your shoulders so they are not tense, and lengthen your spine as you reach your head to the ceiling.
4. Breathe in and out through your nose. As you become aware of your breath, start to pull your belly in on the exhale and expand it on the exhale. Imagine you are using your stomach muscles to pull air in and expel it out.
5. Start to shorten each inhale and exhale, increasing the pace of your breathing. You should hear your breath as it moves in and out.
6. Try to keep the inhale and exhale the same length.

Chapter 12: Exercise & Movement

Start with a single 30-second session. As you grow more accustomed to the practice, you can work up to two or three sets of 30 seconds each. Take some long, deep breaths in between the sessions.

When you are finished, sit quietly for a few moments, taking some long, deep breaths. You may feel tingling or increased heat and energy; this is normal and positive.

If you feel dizzy or light-headed during the practice, you are probably doing too much. Cut back on the session time and take long, deep breaths.

This practice can improve lung capacity, soothe the nervous system, energize blood circulation, oxygenate the body, strengthen the immune system, improve digestion, and create a sense of calm.

CHAPTER 13:
Natural Cleaning Products

CLEANING YOUR HOUSE with natural, non-toxic products can be easier and less expensive than chemical cleansers. Since we use cleansers on our clothes, dishes, and in our kitchen and bathrooms, we have a high risk of absorbing, inhaling, or ingesting these chemicals. Natural cleansers are far less likely to cause allergic reactions, and protect your children and pets from accidentally being harmed by toxic chemicals.

Individuals with allergies are especially sensitive to cleaning products and their toxic chemicals and residues. A clean home improves allergies by removing allergens and keeping bacteria, viruses, and dust mites to a minimum. A sparkling, low-allergen home can easily and inexpensively be achieved using natural products without any of the allergic reactions that chemical cleaners can instigate.

Simple, natural cleaning products are items you probably already have in your home. They are extremely effective and will keep your home spotless and toxin-free.

Natural cleaning items include:

- White vinegar. This is great for windows or as a fabric softener.

- Baking soda. This gentle abrasive will clean tubs and scrub pots and pans.
- Liquid castile soap. This soap is a gentle cleanser for both your home and your body!
- Salt.
- Borax.
- Hydrogen peroxide.
- Lemon juice.
- Essential oils. These are optional, but they are a great way to make your home smell inviting and also cut the strong smell of the vinegar.

You may also want to invest in microfiber cloths, as they are a gentle abrasive that requires less cleanser and can even be used with just water. You might want to consider a glass spray bottle, as plastic can be degraded by essential oils and other natural substances.

A scouring powder can be made with 2 parts baking soda, 1 part salt, and 1 part borax. Use this in your tub and shower to keep it sparkling clean. This gives peace of mind that you will not be absorbing or inhaling chemicals when you soak in the tub or through your feet in the shower.

Don't discard your citrus peels! Use them to infuse vinegar with lovely scent and extra cleaning power. Just fill a jar with citrus peels and pour white vinegar over them. Leave for a few days, then strain the vinegar. It can clean windows, mop floors, or clean and disinfect countertops.

Specific cleaning ideas include:

- **Oven**. A paste of baking soda and water left to sit for an hour and then rubbed off can clean your oven

Chapter 13: Natural Cleaning Products

without all the terrible fumes. This also keeps your food from absorbing the chemical residue left after using toxic oven cleaner.

- **Toilet.** Simply pour in vinegar and brush. Or, pour baking soda in and let it sit for an hours, then pour a cup of vinegar in. It creates natural "scrubbing bubbles!"

- **Cookware.** Salt or baking soda can be used. To create a paste, mix 1 part water to 3 parts baking soda.

- **Bathtub.** Use baking soda and water as a replacement for abrasive cleansers. Then create a shower spritz with essential oils to disinfect. Vinegar can also be used.

- **Dishwasher.** Fill a dishwasher-safe container with about 2 cups of vinegar and place it in the top rack of the dishwasher. Do not add any other dishes. Then run the dishwasher through the hot water cycle.

- **Garbage disposal.** Grinding a quarter of a lemon through the disposal will remove smells. You can also put baking soda in it overnight to remove odors.

- **Mineral deposits on faucets and shower heads.** Put vinegar in a plastic bag and hang it so the faucet is soaking in it. It could take up to 10 hours, but the vinegar will dissolve the mineral deposits and disinfect the faucet.

SHOWER SPRAY RECIPE

Ingredients

10 drops lavender essential oil

5 drops tea tree essential oil

5 drops lemon essential oil

Distilled or filtered water to fill bottle.

Directions

1. Put the essential oils into a glass spray bottle. Make sure you use glass, as the essential oils can dissolve some of the plastic into your spray.

2. Fill with water. Spritz the tub after your shower to keep it clean and fresh.

CHAPTER 14:
Skin Care Products

OUR SKIN IS the largest organ in our body. While there is some debate, it is believed that over 60% of any product we put on our skin is absorbed directly into the bloodstream. Just as we nourish our body with pure water and nutrient-rich food, we need to feed our skin with toxin-free products.

Many products claim to be natural, but still contain chemicals and other ingredients that add to the toxic load, stressing the immune system and often causing allergic reactions. It is important to choose natural products from a trusted source. Natural, chemical-free skin care products are luxurious to use, work with your skin to support its natural renewal mechanisms, and keep your whole body moisturized and glowing.

When choosing healthy skin care products, keep the following in mind:

- Our skin is our first line of defense against illness. The skin has an acid mantle that forms a protective barrier to help keep moisture in and repel toxins, bacteria, and viruses that can make us ill. Harsh soaps that contain sodium laureth sulfate damage the delicate pH of this acid mantle, making us susceptible to disease.

- Not only does our skin absorb what we put on it, we also absorb fumes from anything we put on our face and body. We even ingest products we put on our lips, such as lipstick and moisturizers. The cream we put on our hands can be ingested when we eat a snack.

- Our use of skin care products is layered. Think about how many products you use during the course of a day—shampoo, body wash, facial cleanser, lotions. The more chemicals contained in these products, the greater the exposure for you and your family.

- In the U.S. only 11 chemical skin care ingredients have been banned. In the European Union, they have banned over 1,000. Ingredients such as phthalates and parabens can wreak havoc with your endocrine system and have the potential to cause cancer.

- Your body understands natural products, so it knows how to utilize and process them. In turn, these support natural detoxification and healing working with the body. Synthetic fragrances can cause allergies, disrupt hormones, and just don't smell as good as fragrances naturally derived from plants.

Ready to get started with natural skin care?

The easiest first step is to start with the products that you use most often. For many of us, that will be soap and deodorant. We wash our hands and face, shower and bathe on a regular basis and then apply deodorant to remain fresh.

Keisha's Gemz (www.KeishaGemz.com) offers a wonderful selection of pure and natural soaps, deodorant, and other personal care products that make it easy to lovingly care for your skin.

Some best-selling Keisha's Gemz products you might enjoy include:

Chapter 14: Skin Care Products

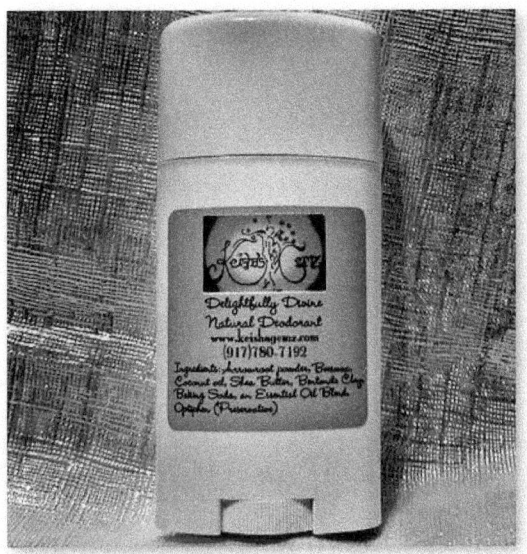

Delightfully Divine Natural Deodorant

This best-selling deodorant is made from natural ingredients. It includes coconut oil for its antibacterial properties, bentonite clay to pull toxins out of the body, and the essential oils of lavender, tea tree and lemongrass, which have anti-microbial, anti-oxidant, anti-inflammatory, and antibacterial properties.

The ingredients label: Arrowroot powder, beeswax, coconut oil, shea butter, bentonite clay, baking soda, essential oil blend and Optiphen (preservative).

Baby Gemz Vegan Handmade Soap bar

This unscented soap is made with calendula-infused oil and fresh Aloe Vera for its added healing properties. Calendula has a long history of use as a wound-healing and skin-soothing botanical. It is most often used topically for lacerations, abrasions, and skin infections.

Chapter 14: Skin Care Products

Chocolate soap.

A wonderful gift for Valentine's Day, or any day, honestly.

This soap contains goat's milk, dark chocolate, and a hint of vanilla.

Dark chocolate boasts wonderful stress-relieving qualities and works wonders in getting you the glowing skin that you desire. In addition, it makes an excellent skin-detoxifier and contains antioxidants which protect your skin from free radical damage, keeping it soft and supple.

Visit Keisha's Gemz (www.keishagemz.com) to see our entire line of personal-care products made with pure, natural ingredients that nourish your body and uplift your soul.

Our currently available soaps include peppermint, frankincense & myrrh, cedar wood, and lavender.

We also offer Henna shampoo bars, and a variety of lotions and creams.

There are unscented choices for delicate and allergy-prone skin, as well as scented products that support healing and lift your spirits.

We offer many vegan product options as well, both scented and unscented variety.

Resources

1. See the Centers for Disease Control and Prevention website: https://www.cdc.gov/healthcommunication/ToolsTemplates/EntertainmentEd/Tips/Allergies.html

2. See the American Academy of Allergy, Asthma & Immunology: https://www.aaaai.org/conditions-and-treatments/conditions-dictionary/allergic-reaction

3. Russo, Marc A. The physiological effects of slow breathing in the healthy human. Breathe, 13. Retrieved from: https://www.ncbi.nlm.nih.gov/pmc/articles/PMC5709795/

4. Dr. Weston A Price, in his book Nutrition and Physical Degeneration, discusses a number of native cultures (such as those in the Andes, Central Africa, and Australia) that consume clay for various purposes. Often they would take a small amount of clay in water to help protect themselves from toxins in meals.

5. Perry A. (2015) Calcium Bentonite Clay: Nature's Pathway to Healing Balance, Detox, Stimulate, Alkalize. Xlibris.

6. Clark, K. J. In vitro studies on the use of clay, clay minerals and charcoal to adsorb bovine rotavirus and bovine coronavirus. Vet Microbiol., 63. Retrieved from: https://www.ncbi.nlm.nih.gov/pubmed/9850994

7. Heydel, S. E. Broad-spectrum in vitro antibacterial activities of clay minerals against antibiotic-susceptible and antibiotic-resistant bacterial pathogens. J

Antimicrob Chemother., 61. Retrieved from: https://www.ncbi.nlm.nih.gov/pmc/articles/PMC2413170/

8   FDA Warns Consumers Not to Use "Best Bentonite Clay." (2016) Retrieved from: https://www.fda.gov/Drugs/DrugSafety/ucm491396.htm and FDA warns consumers about health risks with Alikay Naturals – Bentonite Me Baby – Bentonite Clay. (2016) Retrieved from: https://www.fda.gov/Drugs/DrugSafety/ucm483838.htm

9   Bliss, Rosalie Marion. (2009, November 23). Dehydration Affects Mood, Not Just Motor Skills. Retrieved from: https://www.ars.usda.gov/news-events/news/research-news/2009/dehydration-affects-mood-not-just-motor-skills/

10 Kjaer, A. Dehydration stimulates hypothalamic gene expression of histamine synthesis enzyme. Endocrinology, 2189. Retrieved from: https://doi.org/10.1210/endo.136.5.7720668

11 Overdrinking results in the emergence of swallowing inhibition: an fMRI study. Proc Natl Acad Sci U S A., 113. Retrieved from: https://www.ncbi.nlm.nih.gov/pubmed/27791015

12 Ouwehand, A. Antiallergic effects of probiotics. J. Nutr., 137. Retrieved from: https://www.ncbi.nlm.nih.gov/pubmed/17311977

13 Yang, G. Treatment of Allergic Rhinitis with Probiotics: An Alternative Approach. N Am J Med Sci, 5. Retrieved from: https://www.ncbi.nlm.nih.gov/pmc/articles/PMC3784923/

14 Dennis-Wall, J. Probiotics (Lactobacillus gasseri KS-13, Bifidobacterium bifidum G9-1, and Bifidobacterium

longum MM-2) improve rhinoconjunctivitis-specific quality of life in individuals with seasonal al. The American Journal of Clinical Nutrition, 105. Retrieved from: 10.3945/ajcn.116.140012

15 De Lourdes Lima, M. The effect of magnesium supplementation in increasing doses on the control of type 2 diabetes. Diabetes Care, 21. Retrieved from: https://www.ncbi.nlm.nih.gov/pubmed/9589224

16 For more information on butterbur, including safety concerns and scientific studies, visit: https://nccih.nih.gov/health/butterbur

17 Josling, P. Preventing the common cold with a garlic supplement: a double-blind, placebo-controlled survey. Adv. Ther., 18. Retrieved from: https://www.ncbi.nlm.nih.gov/pubmed/11697022

18 Ashraf, R. Effects of Allium sativum (garlic) on systolic and diastolic blood pressure in patients with essential hypertension. Pak. J. Pharm. Sci, 26. Retrieved from: https://www.ncbi.nlm.nih.gov/pubmed/24035939

19 Menon, V. P. Antioxidant and anti-inflammatory properties of curcumin. Adv Exp Med Biol., 595. Retrieved from: https://www.ncbi.nlm.nih.gov/pubmed/17569207

20 Jurenka, J. S. Anti-inflammatory properties of curcumin, a major constituent of Curcuma longa: a review of preclinical and clinical research. Altern Med Rev., 14. Retrieved from: https://www.ncbi.nlm.nih.gov/pubmed/19594223

21 Zahmatkash, M. Comparing analgesic effects of a topical herbal mixed medicine with salicylate in patients with knee osteoarthritis. Pak. J. Pharm. Sci,

14. Retrieved from: https://www.ncbi.nlm.nih.gov/pubmed/22308653

22 Bhardwaj, N. Suppression of inflammatory and allergic responses by pharmacologically potent fungus Ganoderma lucidum. Recent Pat Inflamm Allergy Drug Discov., 8. Retrieved from: https://www.ncbi.nlm.nih.gov/pubmed/24948193

23 Alsamari, A. Evaluation of topical black seed oil in the treatment of allergic rhinitis. Antiinflamm Antiallergy Agents Med Chem., 13. Retrieved from: https://www.ncbi.nlm.nih.gov/pubmed/23855426

24 Li, Y. Targeting cancer stem cells with sulforaphane, a dietary component from broccoli and broccoli sprouts. Future Oncol., 8. Retrieved from: https://www.ncbi.nlm.nih.gov/pubmed/23902242

25 See www.Foodsafety.gov for information on keeping food safe. Their information on keeping sprouts safe can be found here: https://www.foodsafety.gov/keep/types/fruits/sprouts.html

26 Eteraf-Oskouei, T. Traditional and Modern Uses of Natural Honey in Human Diseases: A Review. Iran J Basic Med Sci, 16. Retrieved from: https://www.ncbi.nlm.nih.gov/pmc/articles/PMC3758027/

27 See: https://nccih.nih.gov/health/allergies/seasonal for a summary of some of the honey studies.

28 Saarinen, K. Birch pollen honey for birch pollen allergy--a randomized controlled pilot study. Int Arch Allergy Immunol., 155. Retrieved from: https://www.ncbi.nlm.nih.gov/pubmed/21196761

29 To view the study, see: https://ntrs.nasa.gov/archive/nasa/casi.ntrs.nasa.gov/19930073077.pdf

30 See the article "Why Swiss Cheese Plants are full of Holes" at: http://www.bbc.co.uk/nature/21059874

31 The Dropping Gemz coaching videos are available free through YouTube or at my website: https://www.keishagemz.com/dropping-gemz-video-series

32 Rosenkranz, MA. A comparison of mindfulness-based stress reduction and an active control in modulation of neurogenic inflammation. Brain Behav Immun., 27. Retrieved from: https://www.ncbi.nlm.nih.gov/pubmed/23092711 and Davidson, Richard J. Alterations in Brain and Immune Function Produced by Mindfulness Meditation. Psychosomatic Medicine, 65. Retrieved from: https://greatergood.berkeley.edu/images/uploads/Davidson-Mindfulness_on_Brain_and_Immune_Functionpdf.pdf

33 Wachholtz, A. B. Effect of Different Meditation Types on Migraine Headache Medication Use. Behav. Med., 43. Retrieved from: https://www.ncbi.nlm.nih.gov/pmc/articles/PMC4600642/

34 Brain Waves and Meditation. Retrieved from: https://www.sciencedaily.com/releases/2010/03/100319210631.htm

35 The New York Times has a short article that offers a meditation on how to be mindful when struggling with seasonal allergies: https://www.nytimes.com/2017/08/09/well/mind/how-to-be-mindful-when-you-have-seasonal-allergies.html

36 Sitting Too Much May be Dangerous to Your Health. Retrieved from: https://weightology.net/sitting-too-much-may-be-hazardous-to-your-health/

37 Tongtako, W. The effect of acute exhaustive and moderate intensity exercises on nasal cytokine secretion and clinical symptoms in allergic rhinitis patients. Asian Pac J Allergy Immunol., 30. Retrieved from: https://www.ncbi.nlm.nih.gov/pubmed/23156847

38 Katy Bowman's company, Nutritious Movement, offers books (such as Movement Matters, Move Your DNA, and Don't Just Sit There), DVDs, and other resources to help counteract a sedentary lifestyle.

Author Biography

KEISHA CHRISTIAN FOUNDED Keisha's Gemz, LLC in 2014. The multi-faceted, healing product line includes natural soaps, moisturizers, and deodorant; reiki-infused gemstone jewelry; and holistic lifestyle coaching.

It was a persistent health problem that led to her passion for healing. In 2007, Keisha's health began to deteriorate, but her doctors were unable to diagnose the cause. Figuring she had nothing to lose, she met with a Natural Health Practitioner who suggested changes to her diet and exercise regimen. When her health and overall well-being improved dramatically, Keisha began to explore how the simple choices we make every day determine how we feel.

She found something as small as a bar of soap could have significant health consequences. She discovered that we are permeable; that we absorb and ingest our environment, from food and air to energy and emotion. This awareness led her to study with various Master Herbalists to learn how plants can help the body heal itself. With various Holistic Practitioners, she explored how our thoughts and spiritual well-being are reflected in our physical selves. She became attuned to energy medicine and is now a Reiki Master.

Drawing on nearly two decades of Special Education teaching experience, Keisha empowers her clients with knowledge. She emphasizes that even the smallest steps work synergistically to bloom into vibrant health—all you need to do is begin.

To learn more about Keisha, view her free coaching series on YouTube at www.droppinggemz.com, subscribe to her podcast Just Dropping Gemz or to purchase natural personal care products, visit her website at www.keishagemz.com.

www.ingramcontent.com/pod-product-compliance
Lightning Source LLC
Chambersburg PA
CBHW050647160426
43194CB00010B/1849